Jt

Happy reading

Parker

No Rumbling With Wheels

Reflections from Country and City

by
Parker Pengilly

authorHOUSE™

1663 LIBERTY DRIVE, SUITE 200
BLOOMINGTON, INDIANA 47403
(800) 839-8640
WWW.AUTHORHOUSE.COM

First published by AuthorHouse 07/08/05

ISBN: 1-4208-4434-2 (sc)

Library of Congress Control Number: 2005902842

Printed in the United States of America
Bloomington, Indiana

This book is printed on acid-free paper.

For Margaret

Contents

Preface

These essays are largely autobiographical. They embody reflections on events and conversations at various times in the writer's life, beginning in rural settings and continuing in the city. They are serious in purpose, but a few are humorous in style and treatment. They offer glimpses of personal history along with comment on social and cultural issues.

Threshing Day

1931

Threshing day is the biggest day of the year on the farm, and we've looked forward to it all summer. It dawns warm and full of promise.

I finish the milking and morning chores with Homer Ellsworth, the farmer for whom I work, and eat breakfast with him and Evie, his wife, and daughter Nina, aged sixteen. Homer is husky and soft-spoken. Evie is slender and quiet. Nina smiles a lot and has big, serious brown eyes, and I think maybe she'll be a teacher. "Today is the day!" Homer says as he downs the last of his scrambled eggs and sausage.

Soon Mark Masterson pulls into the barnyard with the tractor and separator; he's a close neighbor and leader of the threshing ring. He and Homer station the separator in just the right spot near the barn and put into place the heavy belt connecting it to the tractor. Soon the Leamons, Baxters, Treadways and other families arrive with their teams and wagons and Fords, and there's greeting and handshaking all round. Then the men gather near the barn and agree on assignments. Some will drive teams and load the wagons with bundles of grain; others, including me, will pitch the bundles up to them. I can't be a driver because I'm not experienced in handling a team with a heavily-loaded wagon. Homer will supervise, of course.

I go out to the field with Johnny Leamon and his team and wagon. "All right, son; hoist 'em up here!" he calls. As the team moves ahead, I pull over the shocks of grain with my pitchfork and toss the bundles up onto the flat wagon bed. With his own fork, Johnny's a craftsman; as the bundles come one by one, he skillfully builds his load, layer on layer, sometimes deftly kicking a bundle into place. Once in a while we pause so he can tramp the load and check it for proper balance. Then, at a word from him, the horses move forward again along the winding rows of shocks.

I take my turn with the others and pitch for whatever driver comes next. Once in a while young Jerry Baxter comes out with his pony and little spring wagon to bring fresh water in earthenware jugs with corncob stoppers. Johnny drinks from the jug one-handed, which I could never do, twisting his head sharply to the left while supporting the jug on his hunching left shoulder.

All morning the creaking wagons take their burdens from the fields to feed the hungry separator. It drops the grain into a wagon with box bed and blows the straw into a big, fresh, golden stack, while children of all ages view from a distance the scene that's fascinating though familiar.

At noon the horses are watered, and I feed them the hay and oats Homer has set aide, pausing long enough to speak to his team of grays, Ben and Dan, and pat their velvet noses. Then I join the group in the back yard, where a basin of water rests on a crude wooden stand. We brush off the chaff, loosen our collars and roll up our sleeves. A few wear watches secured by leather thongs to the bibs of their overalls. Our faces are tanned, our foreheads mostly white where protected by our straw hats. The first man washes quickly but blindly, sloshing water over his face, neck and ears. In a moment he flings the dirty water aside, provoking a couple of Rhode Island Reds wandering nearby. Then he wipes his face and combs his hair, looking into the cloudy mirror on the west wall of the summer kitchen. The others follow in turn.

At the table we hang back, modestly deferring to one another, but there are places for all. There's a pause while Homer asks the blessing, and then Nina and Betsy Leamon come with heaping platters of ham, fried chicken, corn on the cob, tomatoes, beans, mashed potatoes, and biscuits with gravy. There's laughing and chattering in the kitchen, where the women are cutting apple pie and angel food cake. Nina, Betsy and the other girls wait table; each looks her best for the occasion, aware that some young man may be giving an appraising glance.

After dinner we go to the front yard to rest. Some lie down, leaning on their elbows and sucking long stems of grass that grow near the oak tree. We discuss the work——how long we'll be here with Homer, whose grain will be next, and whether the weather will be fair. Nina stands by the yard fence with young Jay Treadway; I think they're holding hands, but can't be sure. In half an hour Mark puts on his hat, and this is the signal for work to resume.

We go back to the fields with teams and wagons. The sun is hotter now, and we look more often for Jerry to come with his water jugs. When there's a chance to rest between wagons, I sink down on the shady side of a tall shock and watch crickets hurry back and forth between rows of stubble. Clouds drift lazily across the sky. Here, in the south field near the creek, I can't hear the throbbing of the tractor. There's no sound but the whistle of a distant meadowlark, and all is serene.

At four o'clock, when my biceps are beginning to feel flabby, Jerry comes with his pony at a fast trot, bringing ham sandwiches. "Mark wants us to finish!" he calls. The tempo picks up; we'll have to complete the job quickly so everyone can get home by milking time. But now the sun is lower, the heat less oppressive as we near the end.

Before long the last wagon comes out, Homer driving Ben and Dan. Quickly we clean up the remaining shocks, which make less than half a load. Ben and Dan are in a hurry, too; they break into a trot as we head down the lane toward the barn. Our bundles are soon tossed into the chute of the separator. As the last of the neighbors leave for home, Mark and Homer shut down the tractor and separator and cover them for the night.

When the feeding and milking are done, I sit down to supper with Homer, Evie and Nina. We are tired but happy. Homer leans back in his chair and says quietly, but with feeling, what we all are thinking: "Our grain is in out of the weather!" Only a few other words are spoken. To the ample leftovers from dinner, Evie adds thick homemade ice cream. Tomorrow we'll thresh at Johnny's place. Homer will be a driver, and I'll pitch again. Evie and Nina will be there, too.

Our day is ended, and quiet descends. I go out to the walnut grove beyond the barn, where the breeze is cool. For a few minutes I lean against the fence and watch the stars come out. Then I return to the house and go up to bed, and soon I'm sung to sleep by the vigorous lullaby of the crickets.

Hardwood Fever

1932

My home town of Reedsville is in hardwood country. It is a big country, fertile and well-watered, with towns and villages of every size. There are cities, too. But there is a bond between the village boy and the city boy, for this big country, in some mysterious way, has fashioned their mood, their manner and their infirmities. As early as they want anything at all, they want to play basketball. They want to be out on the hardwood.

The limits of this big country are not well defined, but if you have been to Indiana, you have been in the heart of it. In warm weather, Hoosier boys will swim, fish, and ride bicycles as boys do everywhere; but in November, when the leaves have fallen and the wind is chilly from the west, the hardwood fever comes, infecting not only boys but the citizens of all ages.

The lad who has plowed the fields or pulled bluegills from the lake begins to feel the rubber in last year's old shoes; he quits hunting squirrels and starts hunting for a few pairs of white cotton socks. The country peace and quiet don't charm him any more; he wants to go where crowds roar and whistles blow. His eyes lose their dreamy, far-away look and become rangefinders; he turns his back on the open air and looks around for a musty, closed-in place where he can dribble, pivot and shoot. In Reedsville, he wants to put on the "Ol' Green 'n' White" and be a Tiger.

When I was in high school, all male students "came out" every year for the team. Some lacked coordination, and others were just too small. Rejected boys went down to the "B" squad, or to no squad at all. If you made the Varsity you belonged to the Elect; otherwise you were just part of the Masses. But opportunity was open to all, and every mother's son aspired to make the team. To try out was his birthright, and the system was fair as far as it went. If you lived on the wrong side of the tracks or had skeletons in your family closet, it didn't matter; if you had the size and speed and could handle yourself, you were in. In my junior year I made the Varsity.

If you were a Varsity man, you carried a special number that belonged strictly to you, that decorated your back for a little while but burned itself into your memory for all time to come. Nowadays, the mind rebels against the multiplicity of numbers. Oh, I can remember my street address and telephone number when I need to, and sometimes my license plate number as well; but these are mean and of no account. Not so with my Varsity number, for it's a part of me. If I were just coming out from under the anesthetic, for example, and the doctor said to me, "What's your number, Buddy!" I would sing it out happily: "Number ten!"

If you were on the Varsity, you walked around town in a special sweater that added one inch to your waistline and five to your hat size. In these sweaters we were never too warm or too cold. We wore them in class without feeling uncomfortable; and on Saturday night in winter, when we walked down Main Street without any coats on, they felt just fine.

Social life took second place. If other people wanted to go out to dinner and dance on Friday night—-up at the county seat, for example—-that was all well and good. But the Varsity man-about-town, if he wanted to go somewhere and have a good time, preferred to go out on the hardwood and give his all. He counted it a privilege to spend his evening running five or six miles in stale air for the ever greater honor and glory of dear old Reedsville High.

But there were gradations of grandeur, even among the Elect. The idea, of course, was to be a regular starter, or one of the First Five, a distinction I never achieved. We had a number of grown folks around town who couldn't tell you much about the Twelve Tribes of Israel or even the Ten Commandments, but they could tell you all about the First Five and their heights and weights, joys and sorrows, aches and pains. In midwinter, when snow lay on the ground and the fever was at its height, the gas stations and barber shops—-yes, and the beauty parlors, too—-would hum with excited chatter about the

First Five. Sometimes there were furious arguments. Did Willie really foul out of that disputed game last week? Had Spud been loafing lately? Would Sparky's injured knee respond to treatment in time for the big battle next Friday night? The men sometimes expressed themselves in terms both violent and profane, but the ladies were content with language a little more refined, such as "Nuts to you, Gert!"

I'm not saying there were giants in those days—-but I'd be the last to deny it. Each of the First Five had earned his place with sweat and sacrifice. He was not called to the bench without sufficient cause, and occasionally the regulars would go the distance without relief. And so the First Five, in a special way, carried within their bosoms that eternal flame, the spirit of Reedsville High. Theirs was the greater glory and the closer fellowship.

The First Five during my senior year were the strongest I remember. Spud Elliott was the right forward and a dangerous man under the basket. Tall and talented, he was our high scorer and most polished performer. But he had a tendency to shoot when he should have passed, so once in a while the coach would bench him for a few minutes to get him straightened out.

Tiny Overmeyer was our center, the captain and biggest man on the squad. He was a steady producer and good strategist, and decisions he made in the heat of battle usually still looked good the morning after. He was a good student except in English; he couldn't shake off the native idiom, and his corn-belt grammar drove the teacher to despair.

Russ Roberts was our left forward. Living three miles from school, he scorned the bus and rode his bike back and forth except in bitter weather. A rough-and-tumble ball hawk, he got more joy out of the game than anyone else I ever knew, and in a pileup of men he'd be found at the bottom, hugging the ball and grinning. His conditioning paid off. More than once he came on strong with his second wind in the final moments of the game to hammer home the winning point.

Sparky McCullough was a natural-born ball handler, our floor guard and play-maker on offense. He was an only child-—something rare in Reedsville—-and every morning phoned his mother at eleven o'clock, just before history class, to tell her what he wanted for dinner. Rumor had it that he specialized in cinnamon rolls. He was a good team player and might have been captain if he hadn't been hot-tempered; he just couldn't get along with referees.

Willie Burdine was the back guard and safety man under our style of play. He was almost as big as Tiny, and his long arms reached everywhere. Being much in the back court, he was not a high scorer; but he knew where the basket was, and now and then he connected on long shots that brought the taxpayers to their feet. He was steady under pressure and was acting captain if Tiny was hurt or was called to the bench for a conference.

Our gym had good seating capacity, and almost everyone who wasn't confined was on hand before the beginning of the "B" team game, the curtain raiser. But there were a few who stayed at their posts to answer the call to duty. On Main Street, where the wind whistled around the corner and swung the rusty, creaking sign over the sidewalk in front of Grove Jewelers, you could find someone at Lester's Drugs to fill prescriptions; and the telephone operators took turns on the switchboard mostly to handle incoming long-distance calls. Young Doc Ransom always went to the game but sat at the end of the bleachers, and if you wanted a doctor the operator would ring him at number 894, the pay station just outside in the hallway. If you had a high fever he'd come right away, but if you had just a broken leg he'd see you after the game.

At halftime of the "B" team game, the Varsity man slipped away to the dressing room, which was small, drab and dingy. During the week it had served the physical education students, the "B" team, or almost anyone; it had been a place for all sorts and conditions of men. But now it would be a sanctum where none dared intrude. He entered and closed the door. Here, in the company of his peers, he dressed for combat.

When the "B" team game was over, the coach came to the dressing room and gave his instructions while the Varsity men clustered around. The captain picked up the ball and paused for the others to line up behind him, and the coach slapped them all on the back as they filed out onto the floor. There was a mighty roar as the team circled under the basket. The fans studied the players, counting the practice shots made and missed; and the players, for their part, used care. They were no simple journeymen, like carpenters and plumbers, who plied their trade in common places; the Varsity men practiced their profession in public.

One by one, the First Five peeled off their sweat shirts, while the reserves drifted away to the sideline and took up their lonely vigil on the bench, hoping for a nod from the coach. The fans could now breathe more easily, for the first hurdle had been cleared: the regular starters were in fighting trim and ready to go. The signal sounded, and practice was ended. After a final word with the coach, the players were on their own. They shook hands ten-handed, growled like tigers, and spread out to their positions. The noise was deafening, but the cheerleaders pleaded for one last, greater effort. The organized frenzy had begun.

At the tip-off, the crowd faded into the background and spoke with muted voice. In the peculiar hush that settled over the floor, the Varsity men could hear the half-shouts of comrades as they called for passes or warned of danger. They had good offensive strength and were also masters of the zone defense; the hardwood was a maneuvering board on which they faded and shifted, in and out, back and forth, as the enemy pressed the attack at one point or another. As the game wore on and players tired, sometimes there were grievous fouls-——and sometimes tempers flared. But the Varsity man was not deterred. Fear for life or limb could not turn him aside from his high calling. He had a sublime disregard for occupational hazards, and when he had to be helped from the floor he made no complaint.

During the winter of my senior year we won several games by close scores, always pressing hard until the final buzzer, and people spoke well of us. "Teamwork and high morale," they said. With our season record of 16 wins out of 18 games, we thought we were pretty good. We beat a strong team in the semi-final game of the sectional tournament at the county seat on a stormy Friday night in March, and were favored to win the championship game on Saturday night as well. Saturday would be the high point of the year for both team and town. "We're at our peak," we told ourselves. "This time is our time. This year we'll be the champs!"

On Saturday, the wind was blowing warmer from the west and the snow had disappeared, but we didn't notice at the time. The night was clear and mild at the county seat, and a big crowd was on hand from the old home town for the final game. But something had happened to us; nothing was the same. From the opening tip-off we made bad passes. We traveled. We missed too many free throws. Our lapses were painfully obvious; we just couldn't get into gear. The cheerleaders carried a heavy burden as our loyal fans watched in dismay. In the dressing room at halftime, we consoled ourselves and said, "The second half will be better."

But the second half was no better. Willie was slow, and Spud had lost his touch. Tiny seemed preoccupied. Russ seldom got his hands on the ball, and Sparky fouled out with four minutes to go. The reserves, including me, called in to replace them, weren't much help. It was a disaster. Badly beaten, we rode in silence on the bus after the game. We looked out the window, and the coach studied his shoelaces. Back in town, we went home quietly and put our special sweaters away.

But we didn't need sweaters, anyway. Sunday was warm, and Monday the same. At school, we talked about what we would do in the spring, and nobody mentioned that final game. Though sorely disappointed, most of the townspeople were forgiving. "You boys did your best," they said. "You'll get another chance next year."

The change in the weather had changed everything. The fever had run its course and had left us badly spent. We were tired of crowds and whistles, tired of the state of crisis, tired of pounding the hardwood and growling like tigers. We were tired of those frantic, desperate time-out conferences when we all sucked lemons and had to figure out what to do with one minute or with nineteen seconds or with seven seconds. We were ready to get out in the open air. We were ready to go fishing. We were ready for a nice, quiet game of baseball.

Curriculum

1932

When I was a small boy, my biggest disappointment was that it was too late to ride for the Pony Express. I had much admired the courage and endurance of Buffalo Bill and other young men who carried the mail across the plains, especially during Indian wars when relay stations had been wiped out and they rode for many hours without relief. I could see myself clutching my carbine and bending low over my horse's head as we thundered along the banks of the Platte under a fitful moon.

Then Dad gave me an illustrated book about David Livingstone, and I decided to become a medical missionary. One thing I liked about Livingstone was that he accomplished so much without organized support. Clearly he was a better man than Buffalo Bill: exploring the Zambezi would have been easy if Messrs.

Russell, Majors & Waddell had been supporting him with supplies and paychecks.

But medicine was not for me. When I tried to bind up the arms of other Boy Scouts, my bandages looked like manacles, so I decided to give more thought to the choice of a career.

During my last year in high school, I was concerned about my educational foundation and wondered if I could do well in college. Our high school had a total of 97 students. There was no library or laboratory such as I had heard about in other schools, and all we students knew about science, for example, was what we read in the pages of the textbook. The curriculum was fixed and rigid. The administration had little use for music or other "frills," and the day always ended at 3:18 p.m., Central Standard Time.

But teachers were more important than the subject matter, and Mrs. Turner was outstanding. I thought it remarkable that she could teach both math and Latin. We all respected her and relied on what we learned—- or thought we heard--in her classroom. What follows is a portion of it that has stayed with me as a part of my foundation.

Caesar was really from the nobility, but his sympathies were with the common vulgar people. When word came that there was trouble in the West, he raised some legions and marched them over the Alps. The legions carried a lot of baggage, but they traveled with celerity. Caesar defeated the Helvetians and some German and Gallic tribes. He lost only two battles, but several times he would have been captured if it hadn't been for the Tenth Legion.

This Tenth Legion was the best outfit Rome had on the road because it had the most valor. Sometimes the men of the Tenth Legion would gather around Caesar and swear their allegiance all over again. If the fighting was going against Rome and the centurions were dead, Caesar would grab a shield from someone in the rear rank and rush forward so the men could see him. This would rally their courage though exposing his person to the enemy. Then the Tenth Legion would attack from another quarter, and the bodies of the Gauls would pile up on the river bank. The Gauls were very brave, but the bravest of all were the Belgians.

Caesar resolved to proceed to Britain, for he knew the barbarians from there had given succor to the Gauls in the wars. He set sail with many ships. The Romans were met at the water's edge and had trouble getting their weapons down out of the ships. So their arms were embarrassed, but they fought well with their feet on dry ground. After the barbarians were defeated, Caesar forgave their indiscretions but demanded hostages.

Then Caesar started back toward Rome. He was in trouble with the Senate and was supposed to disband his army, but he didn't do it, and he crossed the Rubicon with a whole legion. This was a danger to the republic. However, he couldn't turn back because he had Crossed the Rubicon, so he kept on going.

When Caesar got back home to Rome the vulgars still loved him, so they gave him a triumph. This triumph meant that he had to take a long ride over cobblestones standing up in a cart. While he was doing this, the people stood along the wayside and yelled "Io Triumphe!" because they were cheering him in Latin, you see.

After the triumph, Caesar was supreme, so he began to bring about reforms. But the Senators hated him. They were tired of his dictating and were jealous of him for draining the marshes, so they got him down to the Senate and stabbed him in 23 places.

And so the great Caesar was cut down in his prime, falling at the foot of Pompey's statue. But, even as he fell, he raised his noble head and said "Et tu, Brute?" in the vocative case.

My Flight

1947

I once read a book about mud, but the writer called it ooze. Our remote ancestors, he said, lived in the ooze of swamps along the shoals above the continental shelf. Three hundred million years ago, strangling and gasping for air, they learned to walk on the stumps of their fins. They developed an accessory lung and were no longer simply fishes. They had come ashore.

I've found it hard to adjust to the many changes since then. I don't like change, and I'm never one to take chances. I'm just naturally conservative, and I wear my rubbers when it rains. Never in my wildest dreams have I wanted to fly. But I did fly. It happened in 1947 when I was living for a short time in Chicago. I shudder when I remember.

On the morning of March 14th, I was at home working on my income tax return. The phone rang, and it was my boss at the office.

"We've decided to have you go ahead and close that deal out in Denver," he said, "but time is short, and you'll have to scoot. Better grab the first plane you can get."

I should have known this would happen. For several weeks, by phone and mail, I had been in touch with important people in Denver, working out a favorable contract, but my boss--—and his boss, too--—had delayed the closing, and the deadline was upon us. I complained to my wife, who was working in the kitchen. "I've never been on a plane in my life! I don't trust airplanes. My ancestors didn't fly."

"Maybe not," she answered coolly, "but if you close that deal in Denver there'll be a nice commission, won't there? That will be good for your descendants."

I knew I was licked. Quickly I packed my bag, and my wife drove me to the airport. I hoped I'd need a reservation far in advance, but the agent at the counter said, with a sly smile, that there was room for a single on a flight about to depart. I resented him. The man at the gate was in a hurry as he collected my ticket. Why all the rush? Why did everyone want to get rid of me?

My heart pounded when I saw the plane, and I wondered when it was last inspected. What if it was just a rickety old military transport? I hesitated. Maybe I wouldn't go, after all.

But what if I didn't go? What about that contract? What about my job? What about my wife and children? Dragging myself up the steps and through the door, I anxiously looked round at the other passengers, but they were unconcerned. They didn't realize what we were up against. Taking my window seat, I wondered if they were wealthy; if so, things were looking better for their heirs, executors and assigns. Then the door was closed, and we were trapped. We buckled belts and moved off toward the runway. Looking back, I saw people waving happily from the gate. Well, they were the smart ones; with their feet on the ground, they waited to witness our fate.

I sat erect and took a firm grip on my seat as the plane came alive. Like an angry bull, it charged down the runway with a wild, pulsating bellow. Somehow it struggled upward, and Earth fell away. I swallowed hard. The engines were throttled back as we climbed, and no doubt the captain was saying to himself, as I was, "Well, we made it—-this time." He said we were headed for Denver and would cruise at 9000 feet. His speech worried me; it was drawling and thick, and I suspected he never got out of grade school.

The stewardess approached and asked, "Would you like some tomato juice?"

"Yes, please," I said with effort. Anything would help.

She smiled, knowing this was my first time aloft. Then I was aware of a stream of air hitting my head from above. This crate had sprung a leak! I tried to control myself. The others didn't notice anything wrong, and I didn't want to make a scene. If this piece of military surplus got to Denver, it would be grounded for good.

The stewardess came with my juice. But I didn't trust her smile. It wasn't really inscrutable, like that of the Mona Lisa. Obviously, the airline paid her to smile; she was preparing us for the worst. My head felt light as I recalled what I had for breakfast. A slow panic gripped me. While the captain struggled to keep everything up, I struggled to keep everything down. The constitution of this earthling was about to come unraveled.

The steady pounding of the engines was pressing like a weight. If noise was a virtue, this was highest heaven. The propellers, those skinny sticks, were spinning out there with courage and persistence. But what if they stopped? I kept saying to myself, "If man wants to fly, there must be some better way." I wished my ancestors had not left the ooze. It was quiet there, and secure; everyone knew what to expect. I looked again at my companions in this risky enterprise, bent on getting to Denver at any cost. What would they do with the time they saved? Could they put time under lock and key and save it for the future? Wouldn't the future have its own time?

I wondered about the captain and co-pilot, up there ahead, glancing at their dials and gauges occasionally, if at all. Especially I wondered about the stewardess. She was quite attractive, actually. She could have married some nice boy from her home town—-an accountant, perhaps—-and settled down to raise a family. But no, she wanted excitement; she was as bad as those fellows up ahead.

We were losing altitude! Looking down, I wondered if we'd plunge into some poor farmer's nice, neat cornfield. In fact, there was a cornfield below us. As I watched, the planted squares got bigger and bigger. I felt sorry for the farmer; this flight was our idea, not his. Down, down, we'd go, to foul the checkered symmetry of his art; and he, his shotgun and his faithful dog could not ward off transgressors from the air. Our aerial rubbish would violate his field, his farm, his very home itself.

But wait! The plane was rising. The land began to look dry and barren. Two men behind me talked about the Front Range, and after a long wait I saw the city. The engines were less noisy as we began our approach to the airport. What a blessing! The clowns in the cockpit had had their fling and were letting gravity take over.

But not right away. First, the captain wanted to circle and swoop around. He must have thought he was a big bird like some of our distant cousins.

At length the wheels touched down. We were on the ground! The terminal was a welcome sight as we drew near. Happily I grabbed my bag and pressed forward with the other survivors to the door. Then I was out in the sunshine, on my feet, and all was calm and steady. Old-time ancestral forces surged within me, and I was ready to close that deal. This was my true home, my native land-—this blessed plot, this earth, this realm, this concrete.

Our Kitchen Kin

1965

My grandfather's big family Bible has a heavy binding and weighs eleven pounds, all told, including illustrations, dictionary and concordance. The Old Testament has 596 pages, the New Testament 281. Tucked in between Malachi and Matthew are two ornate facing pages headed, respectively, Births and Deaths. We've always known about the people listed here and thought well of them, and one or two were even considered saints; but there's something lacking: we don't know what they looked like. We don't know whether their faces, in life, reflected hope or despair.

I think we were reasonably well satisfied with the extent of our knowledge until my mother decided to join the Daughters of the American Revolution. Her quest for information extending all the way back to Colonial days yielded a goodly number of ancestors, including a great-great-grandfather who fought in the Revolution and settled in Vermont. She was sure that these hardy folk were fine people, too; but, again, we don't know what they did in life or what they looked like, and for the most part they are now only names.

Over the years, we have gathered the pictures of our later forebears and hung them on the east wall of the living room, where we see them in their Sunday best. Some of them look pleasant, some stern and principled as if to set a good example. They are close to us, and we see them as they are, or used to be. Somehow, though, we pause to look at them only once in a while, usually when we have visitors. They are growing older, and the mainstream of life has passed them by.

Nowadays, public speakers and many others tend to lay stress on home and family values without really saying which values of the home they have in mind. I like to think about those fostered and cherished in the kitchen, which some have called the most human part of the house-—the place where we do ordinary things like cooking and eating and answering the phone and arguing about ball games. And speaking of family, what could be finer than to have in the kitchen a proper place for family pictures?

We can thank the inventors and captains of industry who saw the need and brought us the modern refrigerator. In our house, the refrigerator door measures 32" by 36" and handily accommodates the family snapshots that arrive from time to time and are posted side by side.

This may be our best system yet. Here we see no Births and Deaths of olden days or warriors of yesteryear, but the Alive and Here Now, especially children. In ordinary clothes and characters, they join with us to share the daily business of the household.

And they, too, are hardy. Life is not easy for them, but they will survive. They will endure the many openings and slammings of the door by young progenitors to be and saints-in-training, plus random and frequent rearrangements of their places. Though oft brushed to earth they will rise again—-as soon as they are picked up and reattached.

And so we treasure our kitchen kin.

Little Red Hood

1975

Of all the mysteries in bringing up children, none is stranger than that venerable institution, the bedtime story. When our boys were small, they insisted on a story every night. As soon as they were bathed and in pajamas, they'd settle down on the arms of the big chair in their bedroom and listen to my wife or me read them a tale of savage cruelty about ogres, bears, wolves or witches. We'd do this sort of thing just before prayers were said, and then put them to bed. Later on, if they cried out or couldn't sleep, we'd say we couldn't imagine what was the matter; maybe they had played too hard, or it was something they ate. We'd have forgotten about the churn rolling downhill, the straw house and the house of sticks, the huffing and puffing, and the wicked wolf that sank his teeth into poor little piggy wiggies.

Often the boys called for Cinderella and Goldilocks. I read these the same way, time after time, and they were satisfied; then Hansel and Gretel and the Three Little Pigs.

"These killer stories fascinate them," I said to my wife one day. "They hunger and thirst after murder and mayhem; they take a morbid delight in hearing how the Wicked Old Wolf gulps Granny and scares the daylights out of that little girl in the red cloak. It gives them a shot in the arm every time."

She looked thoughtful. "Maybe it's the age we're living in. They see violent things on the TV screen, sometimes. They expect an emotional wallop out of their entertainment." We'd seen elephants, lions and tigers at the zoo, but the boys didn't seem to think they were as interesting as the animals in the stories.

Little Red Riding Hood stayed with us, but her story became more complicated. We ran across a book that gave a different ending, and the boys wanted to know which ending was right. "Does Little Red Riding Hood get eaten up too, or just Granny?" they asked. So I called a professor friend of mine who knows about such things.

"I'm afraid I can't help you much, old boy," he said. "The essential idea of the story goes far back in the history of the race. There are several different forms, and one is as good as another. The name varies, too; some people call your heroine Little Red Cap or even Little Golden Hood. You'll just have to take your choice. I'm sorry."

I was sorry, too. Without the true text, we had to press on. We decided that Little Red Riding Hood didn't get "eaten up," as the boys said. Sometimes, for variety, we changed the items in the basket that Little Red Riding Hood carried, but we had no more major problems that I recall.

But now a big change has come, and it's my grandchildren to whom I read, not children. They are realistic and much aware of the world around them, and I sometimes feel that my reading of the story leaves them vaguely dissatisfied. Some evening, maybe, they'll say, "Grandpa, let's pretend the people in the story are like the people we know." And then I will have to say, "All right, let's pretend."

The Hoods have a condo in Equity Heights overlooking the VA hospital annex. Father Hood is manager of the data processing unit of the financial section of the transmission department of the Turbolator Division of Monopoly Motors, Inc. Mother Hood is a homemaker and part-time writer for *Equity Echo,* the suburban newspaper. Brother Hood is seventeen and skillful with computers, and hopes to go to college. Little Red is in the fourth grade in school. She got her nickname from the pretty red cloak that Granny found for her on summer sale at the department store.

On a Thursday in the fall, Brother Hood goes hunting at 4:00 a.m. Later, the other family members have a breakfast of juice, cereal and toast. Little Red drinks her glass of 1% grade A milk, pasteurized, homogenized and fortified with vitamin D. Father Hood looks at the morning paper and mutters about stocks and bonds.

Mother Hood brings him coffee and says, "Here's your second cup of decaf, dear. What's in the news today?"

"Market's been wobbly all week," he replies. He drinks the coffee, glances at his watch, and hurries out the door. Little Red goes to the window to see him drive away in his Demon Down-Draft Turbolator with Vesuvius engine.

As Mother Hood starts her housework, low-flying aircraft whistle over the house and rattle dishes in the cupboard. There's an air base just outside the city. "Oh, I hardly notice it at all," she cheerfully tells her friends. "You get used to it. But of course, I have my days. When the wind is in the west and the cadets take off on practice flights every three minutes, it sort of gets me down."

Today the wind is in the west. Mother Hood has been unsettled since 6:45 a.m., when Little Red stood up in bed and called out, "Hey, Mom! No school today! Fall Break! Fall Break!" Mother Hood had forgotten about the Fall Break, when there would be no school on a Thursday and Friday. At ten o'clock she has to have the house ready to entertain the bake-sale committee of the Loyal Home Builders Sunday School Class. This is no problem, but at one o'clock she's supposed to go to the big annual luncheon the local chapter of the Association of College Women, and she hasn't any sitter for Little Red. Last year she could have skipped the luncheon, but this year she's chairperson of the ACW program committee and has to introduce the speaker, the well-known Susannah Smith, Ph.D., whose topic is Simplicity. When the dishes are finished, she grabs her dust cloth and starts dusting the living room. The phone rings, and Little Red answers. "Mother, it's Granny."

Mother Hood goes to the phone and rests with her dust cloth in her lap. "How are you feeling today, Mother?"

"Oh, I'm not very good," Granny says. "Ever since the strike ended, the trucks have been awful——keep shaking the house practically all night. I declare I don't know where they all come from. I never could understand why they built this house so close to the highway in the first place, what with this terrible traffic and all. Well, as I was going to say, my head is stuffy, and I've got an achy feeling all over. Did you read this morning's paper? It's terrible nowadays with all the murders and bombs and things."

"I'm sorry you feel so bad, Mother," says Mother Hood. "How would you like Little Red to bring you a basket of some things you like best? She doesn't have any school today, and she always likes to come and see you."

"Now, I wouldn't want you to go to any trouble," Granny says.

"No trouble at all."

"Now, that's real nice of you," Granny says. "You know, I don't see very well any more. I'm worried about my glasses. The letters seem to jump around when I'm reading. Do you think I need new glasses?"

"We'll talk about it tonight," Mother Hood says. "Right now I'll hurry along and get you some things to eat."

"Granny doesn't feel good today," she says to Little Red after she hangs up. "Would you like to go and take her a basket of nice things?"

"Sure, Mother," says Little Red.

"Poor Granny!" says Mother Hood. "She probably strains her eyes reading the paper about the world's troubles. Maybe she'll need bifocals, and I don't know what Daddy will say, with expenses the way they are and Brother wanting to go to college. We'll have to think about it."

"But you'd better get her some good glasses soon," says Little Red. "You know how it is. The bad news is in big print but all the good news is in little print."

Mother Hood glances quickly at her; sometimes she feels Little Red is wise beyond her years. "I'll get something for Granny, and then I'll call you. So now is a good time to finish your homework."

"I don't want to do homework yet!" protests Little Red. "I've got all day today and all day tomorrow and Saturday, so I can do it Sunday night. There isn't very much, anyway. Every time I get a little vacation, all I hear about is homework."

"But after you get it finished, you won't have to think about it any more."

"OK! OK!" says Little Red. "I heard you the first time!"

She turns on the TV. A man in white draws pictures of her stomach and tells her what to do for an acid condition. Reluctantly, she switches off the TV and turns to her Monday assignment. Soon Mother Hood brings the basket for Granny with these things in it:

aspirin

ham and chicken sandwiches with enriched bread

an organic apple and banana

Product Eighteen with iron, thiamine and riboflavin

"Now go straight along and stay on the path to Granny's house," she says.

As Little Red steps out the door, the sun tries to break through a murky pall hanging over the Heights, and from a distance comes the angry whine of a chain saw. She walks slowly along, stopping to pluck some blue chicory growing between tread marks of a bulldozer that clawed its way through the woodland when houses were built nearby. A blue jay chatters in a treetop. "Hi!" she says, looking up at him. A cardinal sings but can't be heard above the siren of an ambulance on the Belt Expressway.

Soon Little Red draws near to the kindly old woodsman. Seeing her red cloak, he cuts his motor and lays the saw on a stump. "Good morning, Little Red," he says cheerfully.

"Good morning," she answers. "I heard you a way back there."

"I'm sure you did," he says. "I'm very busy. I have lots of trees to cut down. Where are you going?"

"To see Granny," she says, nodding toward her basket. "I'm taking her some good things to eat."

"That's fine," says the kindly old woodsman, "but be careful not to lose your way in this fog."

"All right, but it isn't all just fog. It's partly pollutants."

"It's partly what?" he asks in surprise.

"Pollutants," she answers. "Those are some bad things in the air that come out of power plants and cars and factories. Our teacher told us about them at school."

The kindly old woodsman picks up his chain saw and says, "Maybe you should excuse me, now. I have to get back to work."

"Good-bye," says Little Red. As she walks on with her basket, the kindly old woodsman says to himself as he pulls hard to start his motor, "I declare! It's a caution the way the teachers keep filling up innocent young heads with radical ideas!"

Little Red comes to a bend in the path where there are trees on both sides and several tall bushes--and there, right in front of her, is an old wolf.

"Where are you going, my dear?" asks the old wolf.

"I'm going to see Granny. I'm taking her some goodies."

He steps up close to the basket. "Where does Granny live?"

"It's not very far. It's that little brown house at the edge of the woods right near the Paul Revere Motel."

"Good-bye, now. I'll see you some other time," he says. He turns aside from the path and hurries on a round-about way through clumps of trees and bushes he knows well, taking care to stay out of sight.

Little Red finds it hard to keep to the path. She picks a bouquet of goldenrod for Granny, then throws it away and picks a better one. From time to time she stops to watch the squirrels playing in the trees.

The old wolf smiles to himself as he thinks about the goodies he smelled; he's been hungry a long time. He knows about the Paul Revere. It's on a hill near the plaza where the Interstate crosses the Expressway, and has a bright blue sign over the entrance. Night after night, neon horse and rider gallop in silence above the heavy trucks on the Interstate.

Brother Hood has had poor luck in his hunting, and has only a single dead rabbit hooked to his belt. Finally turning toward home, he is surprised to see Little Red's bright cloak in the distance. She seems to be heading toward Granny's, but is not on the path. Curious, he decides to catch up with her.

Meanwhile, the old wolf has arrived at Granny's house. He circles around it and sees her in her rocker in the bedroom. The back door is locked. He goes to the front door and pushes gently, and it opens with a squeak. "Who's there?" calls Granny.

The old wolf does not answer but walks into the bedroom. Rising from her rocker, Granny screams and tries to run, but falls back against the wall and faints dead away. The old wolf puts on her nightcap, pushes her under the bed, jumps into the bed, and pulls the covers up to his chin. Granny's age being what it is, she will be out for a good long time, he thinks. "I wish it didn't have to be like this," he says to himself, "but I have to eat. I don't much care for meat that's been cooked, but something is better than nothing."

He hears steps on the front porch and quickly adjusts Granny's cap. Little Red comes to the door and rings the pretty chimes that Father Hood gave Granny for her birthday. "Come in!" calls the old wolf in a soft, tender voice.

Leaving the door open, Little Red crosses the living room and goes to the bedroom, but before she comes near the bed stops short. Granny doesn't look natural.

"What big eyes you have, Granny!" she says.

"So I can see you better, my child," says the old wolf. "Maybe I need glasses."

"But—but you told Mother this morning you were having trouble with your glasses, the ones you have already," says Little Red. "You told her you wanted some new ones!"

"Yeah-uh-yeah, that's right; so I did," says the old wolf. "I just meant I needed new ones." Little Red is alarmed; everything about Granny seems unreal.

"What big ears you have, Granny!"

"The better to hear you," says the old wolf. "With my old glasses so bad, I have to listen harder." He smiles.

"What big teeth you have, Granny!" gasps Little Red.

"The better to eat with, sweetheart!" The old wolf springs from the bed. Little Red screams and heads back across the living room toward the open door, dropping her basket on the way, with the old wolf close behind. Brother Hood, coming in from the porch, hears her scream. As the old wolf makes for the basket, Brother Hood swings hard and knocks him out with the butt of his gun. "Are you all right?" he asks, looking at Little Red.

She nods her head in silence and then, after a moment, says in a whisper, "I'm all right." She is still trembling.

"Have you seen Granny?" he asks, looking around. She shakes her head.

"Well, let's have a look," he says. They go to the bedroom and hear Granny calling. Brother Hood pulls her from under the bed and places her back in her rocker.

"It was terrible!" moans Granny. "A big wolf ran into my house and came after me! It was the most awful thing that ever happened to me!"

"He won't bother you any more," Brother Hood says. "I'm sure you'll be feeling better after a while." He hugs her and gets her a glass of water.

Little Red can't quite believe all that's happened. She stares at Brother Hood. "Where did you come from, anyway?"

"I was heading back toward home from hunting when I saw your red cloak in the distance. You were a long way from the path, and I wanted to see whether you were O.K."

"I'm sure glad you showed up!" she says.

"Did that old wolf follow you here?" he asks.

"I saw him a long time ago," she says. "I was on the path, and he asked me where I was going, and I said to Granny's house." Then she remembers her errand and gets the basket. "Here, Granny; I've brought you some goodies."

"Thank you, my child," Granny says in a quavering voice. She leans back and closes her eyes.

They go to check on the old wolf. Brother Hood grabs his forelegs and drags him out to the porch, noting that he is thin and bony. Soon the old wolf revives. He rolls over on his stomach and raises his head.

"You've got no business around here!" Brother Hood says.

"I was hungry, and the ham and chicken smelled good," explains the old wolf. "The hunting isn't what it used to be."

"You shouldn't be hunting around here at all!" says Little Red. "You should hunt somewhere else!"

"Well, I was here first," says the old wolf. "I was born in a den not far from here, but now there's a parking lot on top of it. All the rest of my pack are gone, and I'm the only one left. The hunting was fairly good before so many trees were cut and these houses built."

"I'm sure you're a better hunter than I am," says Brother Hood. "I've been out since four o'clock this morning, but, as you can see, all I have is one rabbit."

"I suppose I'm quieter than you, and I know the territory," the old wolf says, "but I'm not what I used to be. People have shot at me twice, but they missed." He gets to his feet but seems weak and tired.

"From now on, I want you to stay away from Granny and my sister here," Brother Hood says, nodding toward Little Red. "Do you understand that?"

"Yes," says the old wolf.

The old wolf can't keep his eyes off the rabbit. Brother Hood takes it from his belt and says, "Here; I'll make you a present."

"Thanks," the old wolf says. He greedily grabs the rabbit. Brother Hood and Little Red watch as he goes down the porch steps, slowly trots to the nearest bushes and disappears.

They go back to see Granny, who is eating a sandwich and feeling better. "We're going home now, Granny," says Brother Hood. "I'll come back this evening to see how you are getting along. Be sure to keep your doors locked."

"I will," she says. "Bless you, my children. You've been very good to me."

Brother and sister start back home along the path. For a while neither speaks; then Little Red says, "You need to figure out something on your computer. There has to be a way for us and Granny and the old wolf to get along together."

"Yes, and also the company that hires the kindly old woodsman to cut down the trees," he says. "It won't be easy, but I'll try. In the meantime I have something to say to you."

"Sounds like a lecture coming up," says Little Red. "Better skip it or make it short."

"I'll make it short. From now on, never speak to a wolf."

"O.K. by me, Brother," says Little Red. "It's a deal."

The Pleasures of Travel

1980

Travel has provided much pleasure and education in my life. Armed with passports, tickets and travelers' checks, my wife and I followed tour leaders to Europe and other faraway places. Although we enjoyed and learned from our experiences, we had to keep up with a busy schedule to reach our several destinations on time, and often the arriving was more pleasant than being on the way.

Later, we had a different kind of experience. With two other couples, we rented a commodious diesel-powered boat on the Canal du Midi in southern France. It was well equipped and easy to handle—our own mobile home, but with hull instead of wheels. We took our time moving down toward the Mediterranean. There was no haste, no congestion, no noise, and no crime or grime. There were no parking restrictions. There was no search for lodging places and no schedule to speak of. This time, being on the way was more pleasant than arriving.

Returning from all those trips with funds depleted, I sometimes longed to start out again without delay-—this time traveling so that schedule and itinerary were not required at all, and cost was no consideration. Now that I have an acre of land behind the house, that's the way I travel. Now, I can go just where I want, just when and as I desire. It's the journey that counts, not the destination.

On impulse, in early spring, I take a leisurely walk around the woods and garden plot to see how things are going, remembering to check the hive to see if my bees need a feeding of sugar-water for the busy weeks ahead before flowers begin to bloom. On the way back, I pause to watch robins dig earthworms from the ground and gather twigs and fibers for nesting. It's an enjoyable trip. Later, when I go out to the garden to see if asparagus spears are showing or if the rhubarb is peeping out from its winter blanket of straw, I see more birds, and the breeze is more gentle than before. This journey, like the first, is pleasant though unplanned, without reservations or tickets. Many more traveling pleasures follow, unscheduled and unrelated to time or distance.

Baggage is never a problem, as I usually have with me only a bucket of manure or greensand. The only border I cross in my travel is the old fence line between my acre and the house, so there's no delay for inspection, and on the way back I don't have to declare what agricultural products I'm carrying. Since currency is no concern, my pockets are empty except for a pruner and some pieces of string. Rain is no inconvenience; in journeys from garden to toolshed, I'm glad to pause while vegetables and berries take refreshment and have a respite from the summer heat.

Like most other travelers, I'm not far from air traffic. Emerging from the hive, my bees rise over tall shrubs and head off toward the south, flying over my head if I'm at the compost pit. Those returning seem to follow the same course, but avoid collisions by a system unknown to me. This traffic is silent, non-polluting and energy-efficient—-and these aircraft, if I may call them such, are biodegradable.

Traveling from grape arbor to berry patch one day, I was astonished to see my bees beginning to swarm, boiling out of the hive entrance and streaming up the front in long, close-packed, agitated chains. Taking off with circling around and much commotion, they headed for a high branch of a nearby tall maple; then, while the scouts completed their work, gathered in a moving, humming, crawling mass, awaiting the further order of their queen. Though I hated to see some of my bees depart, I knew that I still had more than enough to keep me supplied with honey for the following year and more.

Sometimes I long for more congenial companions than the rabbits I see as I travel from house to toolshed or from there to the garden. On week-ends they flaunt the traditional hippety-hop of a more carefree age, but during working hours they're consummate diggers. Sometimes I find them sitting outside the garden fence looking in, or moving along and searching for a hole. I chase them, hoe in hand, thinking ill of them and their forebears, hoping the next generation will be less aggressive. Probably they, hiding in a thicket by the creek, feel the same way about me.

Entertainment follows me throughout the day, the birds singing alone or in concert, especially robins, cardinals, finches and mourning doves. I don't claim true partnership with these gifted choristers, but some of them have eaten my seeds and suet all winter, and I like to feel there's a certain *quid pro quo.* Late in the afternoon, with more vigor but less talent, the cicadas begin a chattering crescendo that resounds through the treetops, and I stop to listen. I haven't given them any food that I'm aware of—-nor provided housing as I did for the bees—-and I think it's quite decent of them to hammer their bellies for my benefit. They're an interruption, you might say, like the swarming of bees, but these moments afford keen pleasures on my trips. Such changes in schedule, made without notice, add to the enjoyment of travel.

Some travelers nowadays have witnessed scenes of violence, and I have, too. Vicious predators of various types have attacked my vines, especially the dark-brown, half-inch-long squash bugs; on occasion I have caught them in the act and administered the *coup de grâce.* On the whole, however, my squashes have been strong enough to survive on their own. In pitched battles between bugs and butternuts, the butternuts usually win.

Of course every traveler brings things home with him, and I often bring firewood up to the house. It's provided in irregular lengths and sizes by acts of God, but delivery is haphazard and often delayed. Dead limbs sometimes drop part way down and get caught. Twenty feet above ground in one old beech is a 10-foot limb just the right thickness for my stove, and its fall I have been awaiting for several months.

I have a good place to throw discards, too, my discards being fallen sticks and branches too small for firewood. They are piled on a little eminence by the creek, and I look forward to burning them in early winter when there's a light covering of snow. An open fire pleases me more than the fire in my stove, which of necessity is captured, confined, harnessed and driven. The open fire burns with leisure and quiet dignity, dispensing heat to all who would approach. I appreciate that small creek at the edge of my acre, a friend I greet on each of my journeys. But it has a reputation hereabouts as a raging torrent in springtime that floods the fields and woods and frustrates the designs of speculators and builders.

Like all travelers, I realize that I miss a lot. I'm often aware of those who work quietly behind the scenes to make my journeys enjoyable and fruitful. Regrettably, their ways of life and modes of communication are strange to me, and there's a barrier between us. I see them sometimes, but can't know them as individuals. I vouch for the character and good conduct of my earthworms, but the labors of the beetles, millipedes and mites beneath my feet will have to be reported by travelers more observant than I.

Traveling on my own land has many advantages. The drinking water never tastes funny. There's no jet lag, and I've never been seasick or missed a meal. My clothes are old, light, faded and comfortable, and I can always have my laundry done at the same place. I don't dress for dinner, and no tipping is required. Tired at the end of a day's journey, I sleep well, and my bed always feels the same. I notice no changes in ventilation, and I seldom hear strange noises at night.

Sometimes I think I should save up my money to go back to those lands beyond the seas, but the urge isn't strong. Besides, someone else will need my seat on the crowded plane or bus so that she or he can see the sights and take pictures to show the folks back home, as I did. Meantime, here on my acre, at my own pace, I make the rounds so I won't miss anything, and the joys of my journeys never fail.

Messages

1985

One day last spring, I went out to see my friend Harvey, who lives alone on a country lane where grass grows between the car tracks. He's a retired schoolteacher who used to live close to me in town. After his wife, Myra, died, he moved to his new home, and I had never seen it. In early afternoon when I drove up and stopped, he was preparing his garden for pepper plants. "I hope you'll have a good season with your garden, Harvey," I said.

"Thank you," he said. "I think I will. The weather has been good. I hope you had a pleasant trip out from town."

"I did," I said, "but the scenery was the same as usual. I made my way between the billboards and fast-food emporiums. You know how it is. The vendors and suppliers want you to taste their wares. After I left the

Interstate and came down the county road toward your lane, it was better."

"I'm sure it was," he replied. "One of my reasons for coming to live here was to get away from some of the ever-present 'messages.'"

I noted the aroma of honeysuckle as he made a few strokes with his hoe. The lettuce and onions in his garden seemed to be thriving, and the peonies around the edge were budding. Robins were busy digging worms nearby.

"'Messages' seems to be the favorite word of the advertisers," I said. "Some messages are more helpful than others. I'm glad I came out on a fine spring day when nature looks her best. You might say that nature is doing some advertising of her own."

"I don't see it that way," he replied. "Advertising means just the mundane stuff, as I think of it; the usual statements about goods and services for sale."

"I'll accept that," I said.

He folded his hands over the end of his hoe handle and rested his jaw for a moment before he continued. "Ads tell us what to eat and drink and which mattresses to sleep on. Ads are on building walls everywhere, and the city transit buses stagger under a heavy load of ads both inside and out. Only the blind can travel without seeing ads. The product placements in the movies are not a welcome addition. What Benjamin Franklin said about death and taxes is no longer true, as I see it. Nowadays, a few people manage to escape taxes entirely, but no one escapes advertising. Today, the great certainties are death and advertising."

"You've been doing a good deal of thinking, as usual, Harvey," I said.

"I hope so," he replied. "Sometimes I can think better when I'm outdoors and getting sweaty, but let's go and sit in the shade and talk."

He led the way. "This little house is pretty solid. I bought it from a neighbor, and it wasn't advertised. I've done some remodeling. It isn't much to look at, but I like it. I have my own well and pump, as you can see, along with a stove and a supply of wood. But I get ads every month with my phone and gas and light bills. I could get along OK without gas, but I hesitate to give up electric lights and my phone."

We seated ourselves on his small back porch and looked out toward walnut trees and spirea bushes. A beehive stood just to the east of the spireas, well shaded by them. "You used to be a city boy, Harvey, but now you're a country boy," I said. "In a way, you've gone back to nature."

"Only in part," he said. "I do raise a good deal of my food, but I take a newspaper. I skip the ads as well as I can. I've almost given up TV, but I like my radio and the musical programs it brings me."

"I think you're missing a lot, Harvey," I said. "How can you stay up to date on painkillers, hosiery and shampoos?" His garage door was open, and it was obvious that his car was far from new. "How can you stay up to date on cars? Some of the new ones can take you from zero to 60 in eight seconds."

"Eight seconds is a long time," he said. "A drone bee can fertilize a queen in eight seconds."

For a few moments we watched the bees at their work. "We might also mention clothes," I said. "The jeans and T-shirts carry messages all over the world."

"True enough. As we 'walk among men,' to use the biblical phrase, we walk in shoes that were advertised. I once heard of a man who had ads on the soles of his shoes. I think the idea was that some day he would fall over in a faint and turn up his toes, and people would see the message."

"When we first mentioned the ads, I didn't anticipate going this far," I said. "I just thought we might mention the endless contests and promotions, the junk mail and junk phone calls and so forth, and maybe the Channel One program in public schools. Now you've convinced me that about the only place where I can escape the ads is in church."

"The church might not really be an exception," he said. "Excuse me while I get some lemonade that's sugar-free and sweetened with honey."

On the porch, all was serene. The honeysuckle continued its blessings, the peonies waved in the breeze, and the bees worked the neighbor's clover field beyond the fence.

"You were speaking of church," Harvey said on his return with two tall glasses of lemonade. "The central organization of the church I used to attend would hand out fliers about planned giving. They offered choices from a rather full menu, so to speak, of options available for investors. You could select an annuity, for instance. I'm sure you've seen some of that sort of literature."

"Yes, I have," I said.

"Of course. Your favorite non-profit organization arranges for a charitable remainder, or whatever they call it. So your death isn't all bad; your death triggers a benefit for someone."

"Your talk about remainders makes me uneasy," I said. "It sounds too much like remains. What about my remains? When it comes time for me to check out, what will become of my old bones? I suppose the crematories advertise just like other businesses. I've never looked into it."

"I'm sure they do," he said. "The crematory of your choice will have a convenient branch near you. You can be its commodity."

There was an edge to his voice that I hadn't noticed before. "Sometimes I think you're a bit negative, Harvey," I said.

"I hope not," he said quickly. "Judge for yourself. Do people buy from a basic need, or because they respond to a clever pitch? People can be taught to demand what the vendor has to sell. Wants can be manufactured the same as soap and gasoline."

"But advertising is important to our whole way of life, and hard to avoid--like those product placements in the movies that you mentioned," I said.

"Yes, and on TV, the ad is mixed in with the program, as you well know, so one is a part of the other. Now we have the familiar 'advertorial' and 'infomercial'. That built-up area where you live used to be commonly thought of as a city, but nowadays it might be more often thought of as a market."

We were silent for a few moments, and then Harvey gestured toward the sky. Approaching from the northeast, a small plane was towing a banner bearing the name of a familiar soft drink. It passed slowly to the east of us at low altitude, heading toward the city center, and we watched until it had almost passed out of sight.

"That fellow came past this morning," Harvey said. "There's something special going on at the fairgrounds, I think, so that's why he's heading down that way. Maybe the fairgoers are thirsty."

"There has to be an end somewhere," I said. "I think the sky should be off-limits."

"I don't know what to say about limits," he replied. "Creativity is much emphasized nowadays. It's obvious that some people seem to think the way to be creative is to advertise."

"Well," I said, "if that kind of creativity is going to be given full rein, then I suppose there's no reason why the sky shouldn't be good for something. Come to think of it, that little plane we saw can hardly be compared to those big, slow-moving and dignified blimps that float over bowl games and speedways. They can't be ignored, and they draw crowds."

"True," Harvey said. He shifted his weight and gazed into the distance. "I'm reminded of what some people call 'space marketing.' They haven't given up hope of advertising in space some day. I don't know just how it would work. It strains my imagination. It's hard for me to believe that we might have an orbiting billboard."

"It sounds bizarre," I said. "The expense would be horrendous. Would it be deductible?"

"I suppose so. Internal Revenue would bear its part, and the consumers the rest. The consumers are long-suffering and patient."

"When we were young, we were supposed to cast our gaze at Cassiopeia and the Big Dipper," I said. "They were awesome. They were supposed to remind us of the ancient Greeks."

"I know," he replied, "but where's the commercial interest? No doubt the new billboard would be presented as something educational and multicultural. It could be in both English and Spanish, couldn't it?"

"But what's in it for us?" I asked.

He looked toward the sky. "When our day's toil has ended and evening shadows fall, we can look to the heavens and see the corporate message:

Drink Fizzi-cola

Beba Fizzi-cola"

I rose and said, "I'd better be on my way, Harvey. I've enjoyed your fine company and your lemonade. I've interrupted your planting long enough."

"You're forgiven," he said as we walked back past the garden. "There's no hurry, and my garden is on schedule."

I turned my car around. As I prepared to head down the lane, he approached my open window. "You'll recall that Myra and I never had any children. I'm the last remaining member of my family." He smiled. "So I'm the sole remaining consumer."

Losing a Friend

1993

My friend was a common bullfrog, *Rana catesbiana,* and he lived here in the pond not far from my house. Just beyond the pond is a busy highway.

Five or six years ago, I first heard my friend and his companions sounding off. They were young, then, and their calls sounded something like "rid-it, rid-it." But rid it of what? I wondered what they were trying to get rid of. My friend's call was more rapid and vigorous than the others. The older males did better, I thought, with more mature croaks that sounded like the proverbial "chuggerum."

The pond in those days was ringed by rows of trees, mostly oaks and walnuts. The skin of the young frogs was thin and permeable, unable to protect them from impurities in the water, but the trees shaded spawning areas and protected the delicate frogs' eggs from exposure to sunlight.   Insects, including grasshoppers, were available for food, along with earthworms and minnows. In walking around the pond, I seldom saw snakes, turtles or other enemies of frogs, such as birds big enough to eat them.

But changes came to the pond. Many of the trees were cut, and the roar and rumble from highway traffic increased. The algae that had provided food for the tadpoles from year to year was unsightly, some people thought, and twice some men came and put chemicals in the water. They said the chemicals were not harmful to human life. Quite often cans and plastic containers were thrown into the pond from passing cars, so my neighbors and I occasionally walked around with poles and rakes to clean them out as best we could. I still heard my friend at night, along with his fellows, but there weren't enough to make the friendly chorus I had heard before.

Thinking about why the frogs were disappearing, I ran across a magazine article about schoolchildren on an outing. They chased frogs and brought to their teacher some that weren't right. Some had no legs, too many legs, eyes in the wrong places, or other deformities. The teacher, curious and concerned, got in touch with a scientist. His letter in reply talked about toxic contamination, lack of undisturbed habitat, degraded ecosystems and other consequences of human activity. The letter also said that amphibians spend their lives both on land and in the water and are sensitive to changes in both.

My friend, along with other frogs now fewer in number, still sometimes called to me and to others willing to listen, "Rid-it, rid-it." I never saw my friend for sure, but I could still distinguish his voice, louder and more demanding then the rest. Meanwhile, more and more cars and trucks jammed the highway, and the noise and vibration increased. The highway is located to the south and west of the pond, and the prevailing winds coming across it blow over my village as well. I began to get sinus trouble, and some of my neighbors complained about bronchitis and allergies.

I wondered what my friend could do. Maybe he wanted to go somewhere else and find a cleaner and quieter place to live, but found his escape cut off by buildings and busy roadways. His friendly chuggerum came early one night last fall when the moon was high, but it sounded lonesome; I hadn't heard from any of his fellows for some time. His call was not the happy, healthy snore it had been; it was more like a solemn groan. After several weeks he sounded once more-—on a clear, cool night, as I remember-—and that was his last.

Now there's an eerie quiet at night, and the pond is silent.

No Rumbling With Wheels

1999

On an afternoon in June, returning from a business call in the country, I happened to meet a big soft-drink truck on a county road. Feeling crowded, I eased too far to the right. There had been much rain, and after the truck had passed I found my car was stuck in the soggy berm. My efforts to "rock it out," as they say, were unavailing, and I wished I still had my old straight stick. About to give up, I noticed young corn about four inches high in a nearby field, planted in rows far enough apart, apparently, for horses to pass between them during cultivation. That was the way it was done when I used to help with farm work in my youth. The farmer near here must have a team, I thought. The mailbox just ahead carried the name John Fairchild.

In a moment a school bus came along and stopped at the lane near the mailbox, and a girl of ten or twelve years alighted. Seeing me standing dejectedly by my car, she cheered me with a friendly offer: "I bet my grandpa can pull you out!" I walked up the lane with her toward the house as she explained, "My mother and dad are away from home today, and I've come to visit Grandpa and Grandma overnight."

Mr. Fairchild, waiting for the bus, came forward, a well-built man about fifty-five, with sandy hair and ruddy complexion. We introduced ourselves. "That's our Ruthie," he said, as the granddaughter hurried into the house. "Glad to help you. Ground has been soft for a few days."

I watched at the barn while he quickly harnessed sturdy chestnut horses that looked like Belgians to me. I admired them and said so. Yes, they were Belgians, he said; these two were Mike and Jerry. Discussing the weather and his cornfield, we followed the team as it walked down the lane, dragging a doubletree and short cable. Mr. Fairchild reached under my car and attached the cable. Then, at a word from him, the team stepped forward and pulled the car back onto the traveled roadway. Of course I offered to pay, but pay was refused. "Come back up to the barn with me, if you're not in a hurry," Mr. Fairchild said. "I'd like to show you my other horses." So I followed him and parked near the house.

As soon as Mike and Jerry were relieved from duty, we looked at a second team of Belgians, Jim and Danny, much like the first but younger and heavier. We rubbed their foreheads and patted their soft noses. "Four horses aren't too many; we need them all," my host explained, "even though we have a smaller acreage than we used to have. I'm sorry that my son, Ronnie, isn't here. He could tell you more about them individually than I can, and the family groups they came from."

"It's good of you to turn aside from your duties," I replied. "It used to be said that when the weather was wet and the farmer couldn't work in the fields, he was supposed to repair harness."

"There's still some truth in that," he said with a smile, seating himself on some sacks of grain and directing me to an old wicker chair near a feed stall. "For me, horses are hard to replace. I came to love and appreciate them when I was young. They used to add to the social life of the farmer. When he came to the end of a row, he could talk over the fence to his neighbor while their horses rested. Nowadays, of course, most farmers use tractors, which don't need to rest, and farmers often feel they don't have time to talk, anyway."

Ruthie appeared at the door. "Grandpa, there's a phone call for you."

Mr. Fairchild excused himself. I leaned back and looked about, aware of the familiar and not unpleasant aroma in the barn, a composite of hay and ancient timbers plus sweat and dried manure with a touch of oats and harness leather. I wondered how long the barn had been here. Then I saw a quotation from *The Pilgrim's Progress* tacked on a beam above a manger. It was weathered but still legible:

> I love to be in such places where there is no rattling with coaches, nor rumbling with wheels.

I mentioned the quotation when Mr. Fairchild returned. "I read it in high school," he said. "My father always wanted me to read a few good books, and I'm glad I did. They fit in well with what I learned here on the home place."

"So you didn't go to an agricultural school?" I asked.

"I did, as a matter of fact," he said. "I had university courses in agricultural economics and mechanization and agronomy and some other things, and they were helpful, but I thought they were leading me toward a form of monoculture. Many of my classmates were planning on some type of agri-business career option, but that wasn't what I wanted. I wanted to be a farmer. So I never got a degree. After a few semesters, I quit and came home."

"Speaking of your father, has the farm been in your family a long time?" I asked.

"Yes, my grandfather bought it in 1935. It was a good time to buy. The house was pretty fair, but the soil was depleted and the barn was almost useless. With my father's help, he built this barn and rebuilt the house. They mortgaged the farm to do it. It was a struggle. My father finally paid off the loan, and since then we've stayed away from the bank."

"You mentioned the soil of long ago. I'm sure you've built it up since."

"We've tried hard," he replied. "I've always wanted to protect and preserve the topsoil. I feel that if the soil is healthy, then the plants and animals will be healthy-— and the people, too. With much help from my wife and daughter, we have a fine vegetable garden, and Ronnie has made a good start with fruit when he could spare the time. To a certain extent, you could say that we live hand to mouth; what we eat is a part of what we've raised."

The horses stomped in their stalls from time to time as we talked. "Since you're a farm boy, you can truly say that you've 'followed the plow'," I said.

"You could say that," he replied, "and the plow has followed the horses. Horses compact the soil, but certainly not like tractors and other heavy equipment. I have a tractor, but I don't use it very often. If the soil hasn't been compacted, it drains better. It can be planted earlier. The roots penetrate farther and resist dry weather better, and don't need so much fertilizer. At least, that's the way I see it. I don't buy much fertilizer, anyway, since I have manure from the horses and cows."

"You mentioned that you disliked monoculture," I said.

"I still don't like it," he said. "Our rotation here mostly involves corn and oats and beans and legumes. If you had come by last week, we'd have been baling hay in a 20-acre hayfield. What we had there was clover and timothy. I want to work with nature the best I can, and nature likes variety."

"I enjoy hearing your thoughts about working with nature," I said.

"I think it's the best way to go," he said. He mused for a moment. "I realize I'm in the minority. Most people nowadays don't farm the way I do. My neighbors have bigger fields and more equipment. But my fuel costs are low, and I don't spend much on equipment repairs." He paused and continued, "There has to be a way for the family farm to survive. I think it will, but the best way won't necessarily be my way."

There was a moment of silence, and I rose to leave, thinking about the farmer's best use of his time. "You've been very good to me," I said.

"Don't mention it," he replied. "If you could stay longer, I'd take you up to the spring. It's low on the hillside of 'my north forty', as I call it, and it's been flowing as long as anyone can remember. Real estate men want to buy the forty and build houses, but I'll hold it as long as I can to protect the spring and the underground water."

As we approached the house, Ruthie came out the back door. "Some rhubarb, please, Ruthie," Mr. Fairchild said, and she nodded. "I don't like to send you home empty-handed," he said, turning toward me. "We have just a little late rhubarb left, some I brought in this morning. I hope you like it for pies."

"I do, indeed," I said, "and I wonder if you will have red raspberries for sale later on. They're my top favorite."

"Yes, Ronnie will have two crops, one in July and one in October," he replied. He handed me his business card. "Call ahead to be sure the time is right."

"There's something you haven't mentioned," I said. "You haven't told me that this is a pleasant place to live."

"It is, but I tend to take that part for granted," he replied.

There was a pause while the farmer looked out across his land. He smiled. "For three generations this has been the best place for me and my family. I work hard, but I like what I do."

I expressed my thanks, and we shook hands again as Ruthie brought a sack bulging with a dozen fat stalks of rhubarb. I climbed into my car and waved back as I moved down the lane.

The Ten Commandments

2000

Today we hear a great deal concerning the Ten Commandments. However, most of what we hear is not about whether we should read and consider them, but rather about where they should be displayed. Loud and strident voices tell us that we should, or should not, engrave them on monuments or hang them on the walls of public buildings.

Meanwhile, business of grave import is dispatched without a passing glance at any revered or hallowed document handed down from the past. While adversaries bicker about homage paid to ancient precepts, our Congress quietly considers adopting a military budget of 300 billion dollars for Fiscal Year 2001.

It may be in order to ask: Is there anything in the Ten Commandments that speaks to a military budget of 300 billion dollars?

Perhaps there is. It will be recalled that on April 16, 1953, President Dwight D. Eisenhower delivered before the American Society of Newspaper Editors an address entitled "The Chance for Peace" that was broadcast to the nation. In reviewing events since 1945 and America's efforts to work out a just and lasting peace with the Soviet government, the president and former general of the armies said a lot about war. In phrasing now familiar, he spoke in part as follows:

> Every gun that is made, every warship launched,
> every rocket fired signifies, in the final sense,
> a theft from those who hunger and are not fed,
> those who are cold and not clothed.
> This world in arms is not spending money alone.
> It is spending the sweat of its laborers, the
> genius of its scientists, the hopes of its children.

Thou shalt not steal.

Booted and Spurred

2002

One afternoon in November, I went to see my longtime friend Russell, who taught history for many years at our local university. He lives at the edge of town in a small house with flowering trees around it. He's lively and well informed, and I've always looked forward to talking with him. He had recently come home from a long summer in Europe, and I hoped to learn more than he had told me in two or three postcards.

"Come in, my friend," he said warmly as he opened the door. It was his usual greeting, and we went to sit in his library where we could see the flower beds. "I hope you had good weather last summer," I said.

"I did, indeed," he said. "Also, the people were friendly, the train service was good, and prices were reasonable. So my summer was pleasant, as usual."

"Of course you've been in Europe a good many times," I said. "Where would you most like to live?"

"My favorites make a short list, and it changes from time to time," he said. "Now that you mention it, I think I would most enjoy being where people seem to be happiest-—where they feel safe and unafraid. I suppose those are the countries that are high in literacy and education and good public health care. My only negative comment this year is that in one or two locations there had been an increase in crime, but it wasn't serious or noteworthy."

"I've never thought about Europe in connection with crime," I said. "I've always assumed that it had very little. I've thought more about the invasions it has suffered during the centuries, or at least about villains and outlaws on a large scale like Attila, King of the Huns."

"There was considerable comment among Europeans about wrongdoing over here at home, as a matter of fact," he said. "Needless to say, it was mostly about white-collar crime and theft of property by men in high places. You mentioned Attila. The warriors leading those mounted archers when they came sweeping out of the steppes were likely dressed in animal skins. The marauders I'm referring to now, in our own country, who wear suits and ties, are villains on just as large a scale-—or worse--to my way of thinking, though they destroy by manipulation instead of with bows and arrows."

"But Attila was called 'the Scourge of God,'" I said. "We've heard he would stoop to most anything. He would take bread out of the mouths of babes. Would the thieves you mention do that?"

"Yes, by stealing the life savings of their parents," he said shortly. "Attila killed many thousands, of course. These men also kill, though not outright. Attila never had ready access to billions in cash and intangibles, the economic lifeblood of millions. The people and tribes he attacked and plundered could live in part by hunting and gathering, as I understand it. Some had the use of fields or plots that were not laid waste, so they could recover and feed themselves; they were not left destitute. But the victims brutalized over here mostly have no reserves to fall back on. They survive on cash and credit. The men in suits not only steal from them; they terminate or export their jobs and leave them in despair."

The phone rang, and Russell answered. The call was about a meeting of old faculty friends, I think, and lasted only a moment. Then he unplugged his phone, and I was pleased that there would be no more calls.

"How about some coffee on this chilly day?" he asked.

"Excellent," I said.

We went to the kitchen. While Russell poured coffee from the pot left on the warmer, I commented on the small hawthorn tree in his back yard. "I planted it in October," he said. "I often feel the need to watch something grow and flower, something nature provides in its wisdom and approves of without any human plan." With cream added to our mugs of hot coffee, we carried them to the library and seated ourselves again.

"We were talking about reckless pillaging and destruction by Attila's mounted warriors," I said. "Somehow, I don't like to visit parks and memorials where powerful men look down on people from the backs of horses."

"Same here," Russell said with a smile. "You can be sure that most people, down through the ages, never had handsome chargers to ride. Unfortunately, though, some men have found ways to ride on the backs of others." He paused and looked out at the marigolds bending in the breeze not far from the window. "Your comment about horses reminded me of Richard Rumbold, an Englishman who was hanged in 1685 for plotting against the king. He thought he had been unjustly condemned. Under the gibbet he said he 'never would believe that Providence had sent a few men into the world ready booted and spurred to ride, and millions ready saddled and bridled to be ridden.'"

"Very expressive," I said. I waited, and he continued.

"The manipulators we're talking about--those booted and spurred, I will call them-—aren't all in this country, by any means. They have friends around the world. There's much variety within the group. They aren't a formal brotherhood, or anything like that, but they understand one another. Their makeup varies from time to time, but CEOs and judges and prelates and politicians and publishers have been members in good standing."

"You've been thinking about these people for some time," I said.

"I suppose I have," he answered. "From year to year, I'm more aware of them after visiting friends in Europe and talking with other travelers and reading foreign publications and then coming home. These riders, as we are thinking of them, work together and try not to attract undue attention. I don't know how to describe them. They have much in common. I'd say their hallmark is simply the age-old desire to take for a few what nature intends for the many, and their methods are disastrous for the many. They aren't limited by nationality or partisan politics. There's no mystery about them. They operate by privatizing essentials that people need to survive, such as pure drinking water and education and health care. You know as well as I do that they've already saddled us with polluted air and adulterated food and environmental degradation. They privatize for profit, of course. They will destroy forests to make way for their enterprises and the planting of crops they want to be raised." He paused. "Some will go further than that. They will take steps to destabilize the governments of nations that have resources they want. Hunger and poverty are not their concern, and their ambitions have no territorial limits. It isn't just a matter of means and methods. They foster and promote a culture of domination and control."

Though I knew Russell well, I was surprised by his intensity. He paused, and I felt the need to reply. "Of course you know, Russ, the typical response that people like me are inclined to make. 'There ought to be a law!'"

"I know," he said. "Unlike the Huns, the riders we're talking about try to be seen as operating within the law. They often succeed, as they have a power not shared by those who wear the saddle; that is, they often can change the law in their favor. One thing they insist on is a limitation on legal liability for their transgressions. Changing the law is a relentless campaign they carry on with the help of lobbyists and legislators and other agents.

They carefully explain their efforts to the public with the help of laboratories and councils and institutes and think tanks that have an aura of respectability."

"I often see the names of some of the riders and their organizations in the daily paper," I said.

"Yes, you know how it is," he said. "The names of some in the group are familiar, even if all their activities are not. Day after day, in print and on TV, they send out millions of words to explain their good intentions."

"It sounds grim," I said. "We need a way to protect ourselves."

"Every generation must do that, and especially must protect its children," he said. "We need to consider Jefferson's strong words set before us in the Declaration of Independence. Of course you remember 'a long train of abuses and usurpations.'"

"I certainly do," I said, "but what steps do you recommend for anyone who wants to protest? We can't follow the famous example of our forebears who threw tea into Boston Harbor."

"True enough," Russell said. "Let me think about it." Always the perfect host, he had already laid a fire in the fireplace. Without comment, he stepped forward and lighted a match to get it started. After the kindling began to crackle, he leaned back in his chair.

"You were asking about protest," he began. "Given the temper of the times, I suppose a protest would meet a quick show of force by the riders, and that would be enough to convince many people that resistance was futile. No kind of campaign that I can think of would bring lasting benefits. What's needed, it seems to me, is nothing less than a full-scale movement for fundamental change. Others have seen the same need; the idea isn't original with me. In the beginning we will have to make sure the movement is broad enough. Over and over again, we hear people say that everything is connected to everything else, and there's much truth in that. We will have to think about community and cooperation."

He paused for a moment and looked out again over the flower beds. "We will need to talk less about winners and losers. We will have to think more about the future and the future of humanity, especially our children. But of course some individuals and groups insist on winning, and work tirelessly to impose their will on others."

"So then we will need individuals and groups to work just as tirelessly for freedom," I replied.

"Yes," he said, "but more than that, if the movement is to succeed, it must finally benefit everyone in society. It's a large order, I'll admit."

Gazing at the fire seemed to help Russell collect his thoughts, and after a long moment he spoke again. "I mentioned the need for fundamental change. There are two remedies available, it seems to me. The first is well known, but the second is less well known and often misunderstood. Of course the first remedy is to reason with those we've talked about, those booted and spurred, to ask them to listen, to loosen their grip and recognize the need for freedom and justice.

"Well, you know from experience how these things go. You organize and file petitions and write letters and get good candidates on the ballot, and so on, as your cause requires, and try to win by every means available. And you work hard. Meanwhile, communication networks controlled by the riders tell the people, in one way or another, to want what they already have, warning that any change in their status would lead them into danger. You may succeed in a measure, or you may not."

"Sounds good, so far," I said. "But what if all this doesn't work and your strength and patience are exhausted, and the riders are still firmly in charge— what then?"

"I wish I knew more about it," he replied. "Although I'm a teacher of history, the history in this area is comparatively recent. The second remedy has much to do with noncooperation and nonviolent resistance. As you say, tossing tea into the harbor wouldn't be the way to begin this time. As I see it, plans and methods today will have to be molded and tailored to the particular time and place and situation. Much will be required of the leaders. They will need both spirit and strategy, and spirit may be even more important than strategy. They will have to act on principle and serve as personal examples in a struggle where words are unavailing and action is everything. Not many leaders are capable of it. Effective nonviolence may require study and training over a period of years." He paused and then added, "You know the hard part as well as I do. You know what our finest teachers have told us. In all our relations with the riders, we must think of them and work with them as opponents and not as enemies."

"I accept what you tell me about good leaders," I replied, "and I'm thinking their followers will have to be just as courageous as they are."

"Yes," he said, "but bear in mind that both leaders and followers will have a faithful ally at all times, one that will never desert them. It's every man's and every woman's inborn yearning and longing for freedom and justice."

There was a pause. I wasn't critical of what Russell had said, but I was impatient at his measured approach to a solution. "Success in this movement we've talked about could take a lifetime," I said. "There must be a quicker way to get rid of the saddle. What about the people who brought down the Berlin Wall? They got out in the street and screamed, didn't they? And that was effective, wasn't it?"

"Yes, and screaming of this kind will sometimes unnerve the riders when nothing else will," he said. "But remember that the screaming you mentioned was only the culmination of many steps that had gone before, steps taken by those 'millions ready saddled and bridled' determined to gain their freedom." He paused and added, "I don't know of any 'quicker way' such as you are calling for."

He leaned back in his chair and looked out over his garden, where the last of the mums were still blooming. The fire in the fireplace had died. For a few moments I watched the slow swing of the pendulum on the grandfather's clock in the corner.

Our conversation was ended. "The day draws late, Russ," I said as I rose to leave. "Thanks for your warm hospitality and your coffee."

"You're more than welcome——and come again soon," he said as he followed me to the door.

"But I'd like to get back to the man you told me about," I said, "that Mr. Rumbold who was hanged for plotting against the king. I believe he mentioned Providence."

"Yes, he did," Russell replied. He smiled. "When all is said and done, I believe Providence is on the side of those who wear the saddle."

My Comfortable Car

2003

Several times my wife suggested to me that we ought to visit Wilma's Antique Shop; but I hesitated at first, even though Wilma was a friend of long standing. I had visions of wandering through lanes of old books and knick-knacks, and maybe tools and implements of bygone days no longer of any use except to collectors and students of history. Besides, the shop was across town, not easily reached by any shortcut, and traffic would be heavy. But later we went early one afternoon so we would be back before the rush hour began, and found a space in the crowded parking lot behind the shop.

Wilma welcomed us warmly and urged us to take our time as we strolled through the aisles with other patrons. The shop ran true to form, as far as I could tell, but was more interesting than I had anticipated, with muzzle-loading guns, antique churns and barber chairs, ancient doll beds, immense armoires, coal-fired flatirons, and even a cow-hide-covered carriage trunk. Yes, the old books with fine print were there, including early editions of Charles Dickens. Resting beside them were some spectacles. "Those spectacles have stingy-looking wire frames that seem to call for lenses far too small," I said. My wife thought I wasn't properly appreciative. "I think those glasses were plenty good enough," she said. "They're probably just like the ones George Washington was wearing when he saw that King George was a tyrant and would have to be resisted."

We bought one small item, and afterward walked back to the crowded parking area to see the two small buildings at its edge. One housed an old fire engine built on the frame of a Model T Ford. The little Ford looked abused, struggling with many ladders under a long, stretched-out wheelbase as it awaited a call to duty. The other building sheltered a respectable blacksmith shop with bellows, forge and tools including hammers, sledgehammers, tongs and chisels. I wished the smith could have been there working, and recalled the lines from Longfellow that I had learned in school:

> Under a spreading chestnut-tree
> The village smithy stands;
> The smith, a mighty man is he
> With large and sinewy hands.
> And the muscles of his brawny arms
> Are strong as iron bands.

It was a pleasant visit, and I left the shop with a friendly feeling about antiques. Certainly it didn't occur to me that I would ever be back.

Some months later, in early winter, we invited our youngest granddaughter, Cindy, to dinner, aware that we hadn't been seeing her often enough. She's a recent graduate of the university, and has an apartment not far from us. The evening when I picked her up and brought her to our house was very cold and windy.

At first we reminisced about important family events, and Cindy recalled that when she was ten I had taken her to New York, where she had wanted to go for some time. It was her only long trip on a train. "I slept all night in the upper berth, and it was fun!" she said. The chief attraction for her was the Statue of Liberty, so soon after reaching the city we went out to the little island in the harbor with other sight-seers. Cindy struck up an acquaintance with other girls who wanted to climb to the top of the statue. As she was agile and sure-footed, I consented, remaining behind to read again the well-known words engraved at the base and watch the seagulls flying above.

"I was pretty busy when I was there, Grandpa," she said, "and I bet you thought I didn't read the quotation at the bottom; but I did.

> 'Give me your tired, your poor,
> Your huddled masses yearning to breathe free,
> The wretched refuse of your teeming shore.
> Send these, the homeless, tempest-tost to me.
> I lift my lamp beside the golden door!'"

She mentioned her major study at the university, a double major, but I couldn't remember the names. In my day, a student had one major, something you could get hold of, maybe history or philosophy or chemistry. Cindy's double major sounded like science and the humanities, and she seemed to feel there was no conflict. Then she told us about her new job at the children's home not far away. It was obvious that she was dedicated to caring for the children there, and one of her concerns was the lack of clean air. One child she spoke of was Caroline, who had to fight for her breath, and another was little Billy, who had asthma. Her earnest and sincere comments were sometimes about industrial plants of various kinds, but mostly about the heavy motor traffic. We had a fine visit with Cindy. It seemed clear that she would do well and have a good future in her work, and it was rather late when our conversation was ended and I took her home.

At bedtime, I realized that I might have eaten too much for dinner. I was thinking about Cindy and the children when I drifted off to sleep. Images without any logic kept crowding in, and they were not restful. And a dream began.

In my dream, it was a Saturday morning in the fall. I walked two blocks from my house and boarded the train at my regular station, pleased to find that a city-wide commuter rail system, long discussed but never planned, was now completed and in full operation. The air was clear and bracing. Several young people boarded also, some with bicycles. Cindy boarded at the next stop, and it seemed entirely in order for her to take me to the antique shop where I had already been. More people with bicycles boarded from time to time. They would go to the end of the line, Cindy explained, there to gather for a 50-mile rally in the hills. The train seemed to cruise without effort. We were elevated for a time, but later were on the surface, and whizzed through crossings where cars waited for the gates to rise.

"The motorists are very patient," I said.

"Well, maybe more patient on Saturday than on other days," she said. She commented in a matter-of-fact way about the autos at the crossings, her description of power sources making everything sound electric, though the only source I was really familiar with was gasoline. In only fifteen minutes, it seemed, we were slowing for the proper stop.

"We made good time today," I said.

"Yes, as usual," Cindy said. "We couldn't get along well without the rails. When you were young-—or maybe when Great Grandpa was young—-a man could pitch his tent out on the prairie, so to speak. But things are different, now. A lot of people are like me. They live and work stacked up in cities, and they need a quick and clean way to get around. Cars are nice for running errands, sometimes, and for going on vacation. But they aren't the best answer when you have to go to work on time and get back on time every day in all kinds of weather, and thousands of other people are doing the very same thing."

We alighted and walked a block and a half to the antique shop, entering this time at the front. Wilma greeted us, and we took our time so Cindy could see it all—-guns, churns, doll beds, flatirons and whatnot—-along with Dickens and eyeglasses. Then I remembered the blacksmith shop and fire engine, so we went out the back entrance, where my wife and I had been before. Two or three cars were in the parking lot, along with a number of visitors. I looked first at the smithy to check out the forge, bellows and tools, wishing the smith were there; then at the plucky little Ford hook-and-ladder.

But there was a third building nearby. It housed an auto, and I went to take a look, unprepared for the shock awaiting me. It was my car! *My car!* I couldn't accept what I saw. For the public, the make, model and other details were listed; but I knew more. That small crease in the right quarter panel was still there, and the nick in the license-plate holder that I had made one day when my screwdriver slipped. I checked everything carefully, and there was no mistake. The car was mine.

"They can't do this to me!" I protested to Cindy. "It's a travesty! My car is not a relic! It's not a museum piece like a smithy and a Model T Ford!" I looked around, trying to keep my voice down, but no one had noticed me.

Cindy was unmoved. "It can't be helped, Grandpa. Each one belongs to its own era. Each had its time of greatest usefulness."

"My car has everything on it," I said. "It's got speed control and climate control and airbags and all the safety things. It's full-sized and comfortable; you know that. You've ridden in it, yourself!"

"But that isn't the whole story, Grandpa," she answered. "You haven't mentioned what comes out of its tailpipe."

Cindy eased me away from the exhibits. We went down the driveway, then walked back the block and a half to the rail station and seated ourselves. "We've talked about sources of power," Cindy reminded me as we waited. "One generation discovers oil; another discovers the limitations of oil."

It was hard to argue with Cindy. She and I had always been friends. I didn't want to protest too much, so I asked her about the little folks at the children's home. "They're getting the best of care," she said, "but some have problems because of poor air quality, as I've mentioned before. Everybody gets just one set of lungs and has to take care of them."

"You've had a concern about clean air for a long time," I said.

"Yes, and I often think about our trip to New York," she replied. "I'm glad you took me, and I'm grateful. And I'm grateful to the Statue of Liberty, actually. I believe Emma Lazarus had it about right:

> 'Give me your tired, your poor,
> Your huddled masses yearning to breathe free…'"

"But I don't think that was really the point she was trying to make," I said. "She wasn't thinking about power plants and cars; she was thinking about freedom from oppression."

"But isn't pollution a form of oppression?" she asked.

The platform stirred with activity as people came with packages and children. The train arrived, and we found seats. I looked out the window, but the fall colors didn't seem bright any more. I thanked Cindy for taking me to the antique shop. In a few minutes we had arrived at her stop. She smiled and said something about getting together again, but I couldn't remember what it was. Then she kissed me good-bye and was gone.

I leaned back to think. My stop would be next, in three minutes. My thoughts about Cindy were all in a jumble: Dickens—-eyeglasses-—people stacked up-—huddled masses-—little Billy—-wretched refuse-—power sources-—the indignities heaped upon my car. Then the train trip ended and the images faded away.

The dream ended. I was at home, now. It was dark, and I was awake. I began to think about that other trip, the real one we took to New York when Cindy was ten. We were on that island in the harbor with seagulls flying above. The statue was before me, and the lady was lifting her lamp. Cindy was climbing to the top, and maybe already was having thoughts about freedom.

Acknowledgments

In preparing these reflections, I am mindful of faithful friends in the Writers' Center of Indiana, with some of whom I met from time to time so we could read one another's work. Their help has been invaluable. Class members and leaders I remember most are Steve Craig, Joyce Flight, Miriam Guidero, Leila Peters, Jim Powell, Barbara Shoup and Robin Yates; also Charlotte Sargeant and Wilfred H. DeWitt, both now deceased.

Many others have encouraged me, and special thanks are due to Faithe Wempen for her pointers on the use of my computer.

Last and always, I am immensely grateful to my wife and family for their strong support.

About the Writer

Parker Pengilly was born in Wisconsin but grew up in small towns in Indiana. He attended DePauw University on a scholarship.

After law school at Indiana University, he served three and a half years in the Navy, first in the Office of Naval Intelligence and later as communications officer on an aircraft carrier in the Pacific. After naval service, he was employed for five years in the legal department of American Telephone and Telegraph Company. He then practiced law in Indianapolis before retiring.

His travels have permitted him to see much of the United States, including Alaska and Hawaii. He has also traveled in Europe, the South Pacific, Southeast Asia, Australia and New Zealand.

His hobbies are reading, gardening and beekeeping.

He has three sons and lives with his wife, Margaret, in Indianapolis.

Printed in the United States
57274LVS00007B/6

9 781420 844344